D1123287

 ZONDER**kidz**™

Original edition published in Denmark under the title Seek and Find in the Bible by Scandinavia Publishing House, Copenhagen, Denmark Copyright © Scandinavia Publishing House.

Seek and Find Bible Stories
Copyright © 2008 by Zondervan
Text by Carl Anker Mortensen
Illustrated by José Pérez Montero

Published by license with Scandinavia Publishing House.
Requests for information should be addressed to:
Zonderkidz, Grand Rapids, Michigan 49530

Library of Congress Catalog Card Number 2007941628

All Scripture quotations unless otherwise noted are taken from the *Holy Bible: New International Version*®. NIV®. Copyright © 1973, 1978, 1984 by International Bible Society. Used by permission of Zondervan. All rights reserved.

All rights reserved. No part of this publication may be reproduced, stored in a retrieval system, or transmitted in any form or by any means—electronic, mechanical, photocopy, recording, or any other—except for brief quotations in printed reviews, without the prior permission of the publisher.

Zonderkidz is a trademark of Zondervan.

Cover design: Mark Veldheer
Interior design: Nils Glistrup
Illustrations copyright © José Pérez Montero

Printed in Singapore

08 09 10 11 • 6 5 4 3 2 1

SEEK AND FIND
BIBLE STORIES

Written by **Carl Anker Mortensen**

Illustrated by **José Pérez Montero**

ZONDERVAN.com/
AUTHORTRACKER
follow your favorite authors

THE OLD TESTAMENT

CONTENTS

WHO IS MIKE?

Mike is a lot of fun to be with. When he reads his Bible, something special happens. He imagines the stories so vividly, that the stories start to fill the room! Suddenly, Mike shows up in the middle of the action. In every exciting Bible story, you'll find Mike looking for adventure.

Mike is mischievous. He likes to hide and make other people look for him. He disappears into scenery and among crowds or groups of animals. But Mike may be hard to find once he gets involved in what's happening. Be on the lookout for Mike in each story.

God Creates the World

God is busy creating the animals when Mike shows up. Mike has never even seen most of these animals. Do you recognize the one he's sitting on? What is it called? Mike can see that people have not been created yet. In six days God created the earth and everything in it. Then he rested on the seventh day.

Questions

1. What is your favorite animal?

2. Can you find the family of lions?

3. What is the largest elephant doing?

4. How many of the animals do you recognize?

5. What are they called?

6. What would you call them, if you had Adam's job of naming the animals?

Read

Genesis 1:24–25

God made the wild animals according to their kinds, the livestock according to their kinds, and all the creatures that move along the ground according to their kinds. And God saw that it was good.

—Genesis 1:25

Noah Builds an Ark

Here is Noah. God has given him the job of building a large boat. It's called an ark. When the rain starts falling, every living creature who doesn't make it into the ark will drown. It is God's punishment for those who choose not to listen to him and follow his ways. Can you see Noah? He is helping two of every kind of animal into the ark. Noah's family is going to be safe onboard. Where has Mike gone off to?

Questions

1. Find Noah. What do you think he is doing?

2. How many different animals are on their way into the ark?

3. How are the parrots getting in?

4. What makes you think that Noah is expecting the rain to start soon?

5. Find Noah's wife. What is she afraid of?

6. Have you ever made something that could float?

Read

Genesis 6:13–22

I am going to bring floodwaters on the earth to destroy all life under the heavens, every creature that has the breath of life in it ... But I will establish my covenant with you, and you will enter the ark.

—*Genesis 6:17–18*

Arguing at the Tower of Babel

There are lots of people here, all gathered together in one place. The people are trying to build a tower so high that it reaches clear up to heaven. This does not please God. He stops them by suddenly making them speak many different languages at one time. No one can understand what the person next to him is saying. The people can't build the tower together. Mike is looking for someone who speaks English. Can you find him?

Questions

1. Can you find the missing horseshoe?

2. What game do you think the children are playing with the camel?

3. Find the man with the bad foot. What happened?

4. What are they building the tower out of?

5. Can you say anything in a different language?

Read

Genesis 11:1–9

Come, let us build ourselves a city, with a tower that reaches to the heavens, so that we may make a name for ourselves and not be scattered over the face of the whole earth.

—*Genesis 11:4*

Israelites Cry in Egypt

The Israelites are the people of God. They come from the land of Israel. One time when they had nothing to eat in their country, they traveled all the way to Egypt to find food. After many years in Egypt, many, many children, grandchildren and great-grandchildren were born. Pharaoh, the king of Egypt, made slaves out of the people of Israel. Can you see the whips he used on them? The Israelites cry out to God to help them. Mike is hiding from the slave masters. You probably would too, if you were there.

Questions

1. What are the animals doing?

2. Find all the Egyptians with whips. How many are there?

3. Look for other Egyptians. What are they doing?

4. What kind of work do the women do?

5. Do the children work hard too?

6. Who is not working? Really?

Read

Exodus 1:7–14

The Israelites groaned in their slavery and cried out, and their cry for help because of their slavery went up to God.

—Exodus 2:23

Escape to Freedom

When Moses led the people of Israel out of Egypt, king Pharaoh sent the Egyptian army to bring them back. God rescued all the men, women, and children by helping them cross the Red Sea through a narrow pathway of dry land. When the Egyptian army followed through, the sea walls collapsed and all the soldiers drowned. God's people were safe on the other side. Mike is cheering for the Israelites. Can you find him?

Questions

1. Can you find the artist painting a picture? What is he painting?

2. Find the happy Israelites. Why do you think they are so happy?

3. Look for the boy on the scooter. What do you think he's thinking about?

4. Which way do the Israelites go now?

Read

Exodus 14:21–30

The water flowed back and covered the chariots and horsemen—the entire army of Pharaoh that had followed the Israelites into the sea. Not one of them survived.

—Exodus 14:28

War Against the Amalekites

There is a war going on here. The enemy is a tribe called the Amalekites. God's people, the people of Israel, are fighting hard. Mike wants to see who will win. He is watching the man named Moses who is holding his hands in the air. As long as Moses holds his arms up, the Israelites will keep on winning. Guess who is helping them win.

Questions

1. Can you find the man taking a shower?

2. Can you find the warrior pleading for mercy for his life?

3. Can you find the wagons with first aid items?

4. Look for the fire. Do you think the tent will burn down?

5. Look for the vender. What is he selling?

Read

Exodus 17:8–13

As long as Moses held up his hands, the Israelites were winning, but whenever he lowered his hands, the Amalekites were winning.

—*Exodus 17:11*

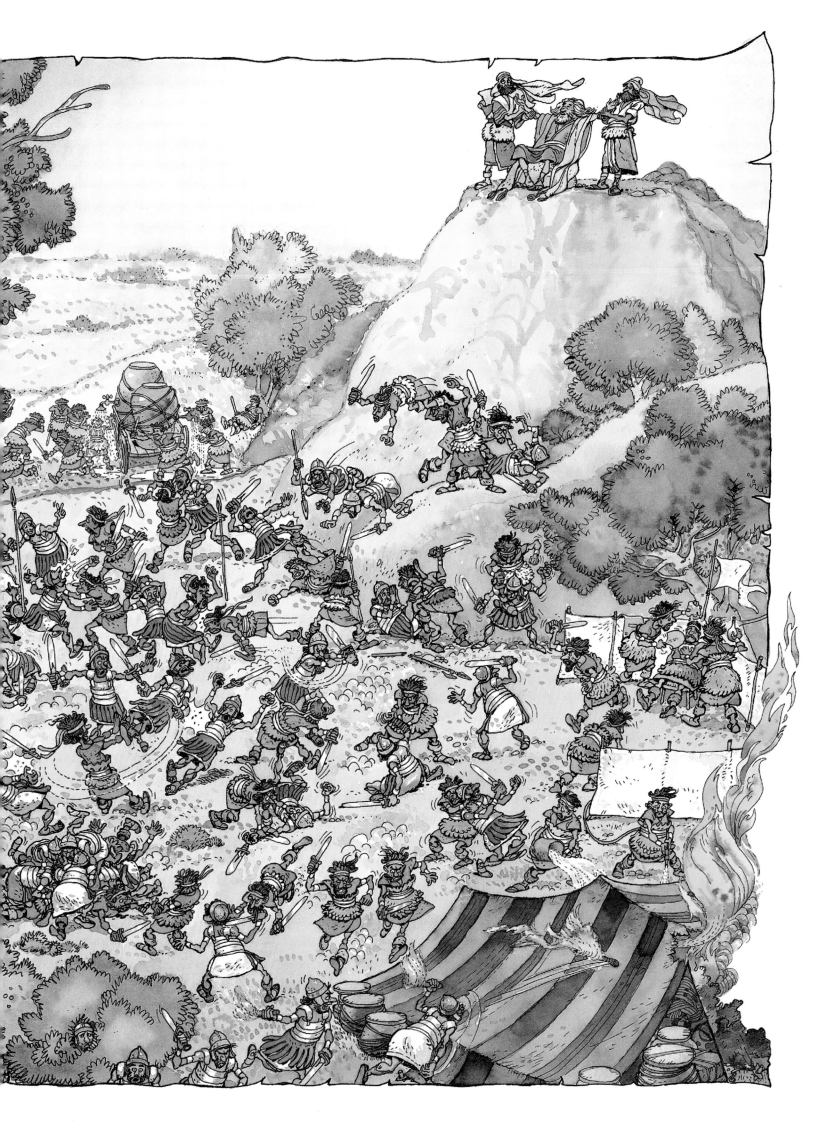

Eating Manna in the Desert

The Israelites are on a long journey to their own country. They have been camping in tents and wandering in the desert for a long time. They've just discovered that God has provided a new kind of food for them. It is lying on the ground and looks like snow. But it's really a type of bread called manna. Mike thinks it tastes good.

Questions

1. How can you tell that it is not winter?

2. Can you find the man with skis and ski poles?

3. Do the animals also eat the manna?

4. How many happy people can you find?

5. When was the last time you tried a new food?

Read

Exodus 16:12–16

Thin flakes like frost on the ground appeared on the desert floor ... Moses said to them, "It is the bread the Lord has given you to eat."

—*Exodus 16:14–15*

The Fall of Jericho

The Israelites are back in Israel in a town called Jericho. Can you see what is happening? God told his people what to do. They walked around the town for six days. Today is the seventh day. After the seventh time around, they shout with all their might and blow loudly on their horns. When they do that, God makes the big wall around the town crumble and fall down. Mike looks scared. Is he running away?

Questions

1. How many different trumpets can you find? Can you find more than eight?

2. What else is making noise?

3. Who is walking at the front of the army?

4. Can you find any children in the crowd?

5. How many times have they walked around the walls so far?

6. Why did Jericho have a wall around it?

Read

Joshua 6:1–20

When the trumpets sounded, the people shouted, and at the sound of the trumpet, when the people gave a loud shout, the wall collapsed.

—*Joshua 6:20*

Life in Israel

Back in Israel, the people of God are living happily in freedom. They are no longer living like they lived as slaves in Egypt. They love to work here, making their fields grow and bear fruit. They are working on the grape harvest now. They gather grapes in large baskets. Mike is enjoying himself. Do you like grapes too?

Questions

1. Find the men in the huge basin. What are they doing?

2. Find some children. Are they working on the grape harvest too?

3. What kind of working animals do you find?

4. What do you think they use the pitchers for?

5. Find the man relaxing. Do you ever relax when other people are doing chores?

Read

Joshua 24:13

When the LORD your God brings you into the land he swore to your fathers . . . then when you eat and are satisfied, be careful that you do not forget the LORD, who brought you out of Egypt.

—*Deuteronomy 6:10–12*

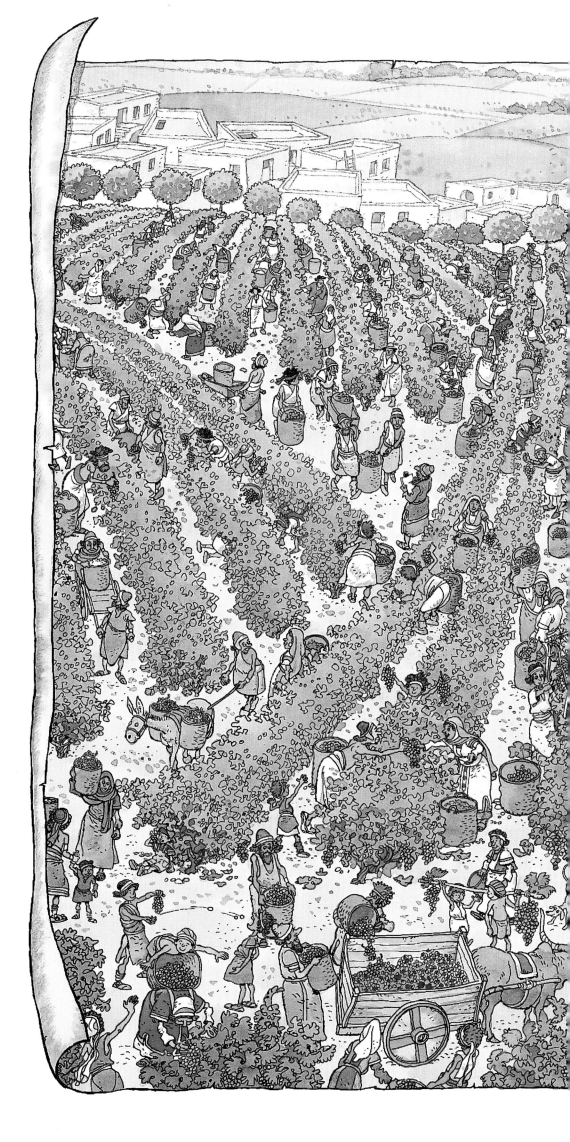

20

Strong Samson

Most of these people are Philistines, the worst enemies of God's people, the Israelites. But the man standing between the columns is not a Philistine. His name is Samson. The Philistines have poked his eyes out. When Samson's hair is long, as it is now, God makes him strong. Whoops, can you see Mike is sneaking away? In a moment, Samson will push the columns down so the entire building crashes down. That is Samson's way of defeating the Philistines.

Questions

1. Look for the balloon man. How many balloons do you see?

2. Find the two photographers. When do you see people taking a lot of pictures?

3. Locate the people hiding under a table.

4. Find the lady wearing glasses.

5. Find the man who is kneeling.

6. Have you found anyone smiling?

Read

Judges 16:23–30

Samson said to the servant who held his hand, "Put me where I can feel the pillars that support the temple, so that I may lean against them." Now the temple was crowded with men and women; all the rulers of the Philistines were there, and on the roof were about three thousand men and women watching Samson perform. Then Samson prayed to the LORD, "O Sovereign LORD, remember me. O God, please strengthen me just once more . . ." Then Samson reached toward the two central pillars on which the temple stood . . . Then he pushed with all his might, and down came the temple on the rulers and all the people in it. Thus he killed many more when he died than while he lived.

—*Judges 16:26–30*

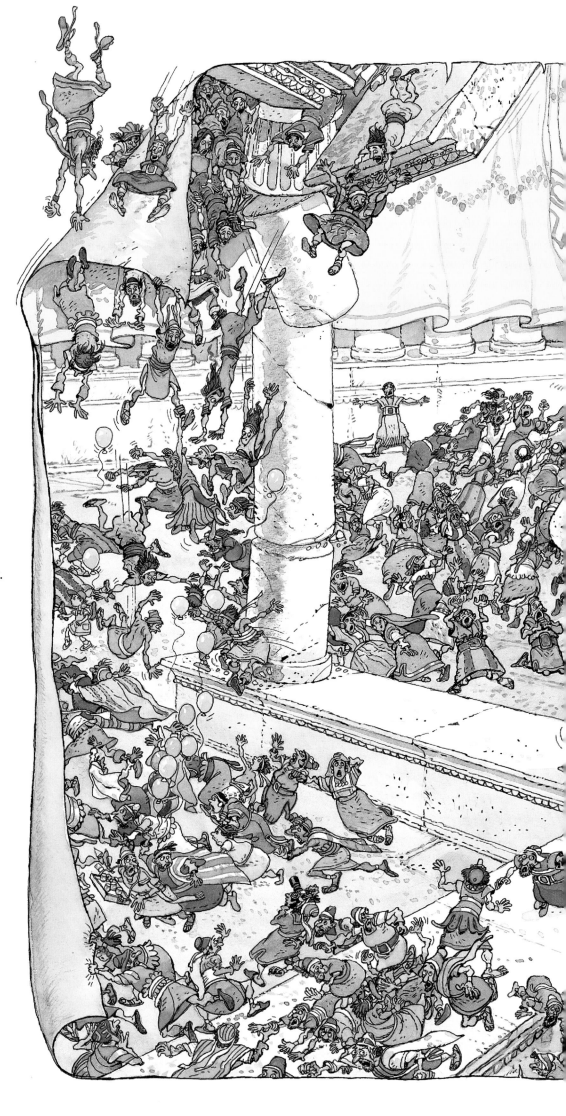

David Fights Goliath

Here lies Goliath, a giant soldier from the Philistine army. He no longer swears at God or makes jokes about David, the shepherd boy. David has knocked him down with a slingshot and one stone. The stone hit Goliath right in the forehead. Because of David's strong faith in God, he won this battle that everyone thought he would lose. Now the Israelites are jumping for joy—so is Mike.

Questions

1. Can you see the pile of weapons? Why do you think the Israelites left them there?

2. Why do you think one of the men is leaving the picture?

3. David is holding Goliath's sword. What do you think he will do with it?

4. How can you tell who the Israelites are?

5. Find the Philistine man biting his fingernails. What is he afraid of?

Read

1 Samuel 17:32–54

Reaching into his bag and taking out a stone, he slung it and struck the Philistine on the forehead. The stone sank into his forehead, and he fell facedown on the ground. So David triumphed over the Philistine with a sling and a stone.

—1 Samuel 17:49–50

David Takes the Ark of the Covenant

Mike has arrived at a party to celebrate bringing the ark of the covenant back to Jerusalem, the capital of Israel. David is king now (he is the first one in line), dancing for joy. The pure gold ark is the most important thing to the Israelites. It is kept in the most holy place, the temple. The Israelites believed that where the ark is, God lives. Now God will be in the middle of the holy city of Jerusalem. Everyone is happy. Can you see Mike dancing too?

Questions

1. How many different musical instruments can you find? There are eight.

2. Can you find a funny bicycle?

3. Can you find the tourist guide?

4. What are they using for a Frisbee?

5. Find the kids playing wheelbarrow. Have you ever played wheelbarrow?

6. Why would you jump or dance for joy?

Read

2 Samuel 6:1–19

David danced before the LORD with all his might, while he and the entire house of Israel brought up the ark of the Lord with shouts and the sound of trumpets.

—*2 Samuel 6:14–15*

Building God's Temple

These people are building a temple. Before King David died, he had gathered all the materials needed. His son, Solomon, is king now. God told Solomon exactly how to build the temple. It will bring great glory to God. It is going to be big. It's good there are many construction workers and craftsmen to do the work. Mike won't be much help. But he's going to hang around and watch.

Questions

1. Can you find workers on roller skates?

2. How many different animals are being used in the work?

3. Look for the line of workers carrying stones. How many are there?

4. How did they find out what the temple should look like?

5. Why is smoke coming out of the chimney?

6. What else was Solomon famous for?

Read

1 Kings 6

In the eleventh year in the month of Bul, the eighth month, the temple was finished in all its details according to its specifications. He had spent seven years building it.

—*1 Kings 6:38*

Jerusalem's Walls

Have you ever seen so many builders working on a project? The walls of Jerusalem have been destroyed by Israel's enemies and the gates were burned to the ground. Mike is speaking with a man named Nehemiah. Nehemiah is directing the whole operation, rebuilding the giant walls of Jerusalem. It is important for Israel to rebuild the walls so they will be safe from their enemies.

Questions

1. Can you find the man carrying his donkey on his shoulders?

2. Where is the man on a skateboard?

3. Can you find a mouse?

4. Can you find the boy pulling a cat by the tail?

5. Can you find a kangaroo in the picture?

6. How many different animals can you find? How about seven?

7. Can you point out the man with a sword in his belt?

Read

Nehemiah 3:1–32

So the wall was completed.... When all our enemies heard about this, all the surrounding nations were afraid and lost their self-confidence, because they realized that this work had been done with the help of our God.

—*Nehemiah 6:15–16*

Here are some of the things Mike found on his journey through the Old Testament. Unfortunately, he can't remember where he found them. Can you help him out?

Questions

 Is this a flower? If not, what is it?

 What kind of animal is this?

 This will be extremely hard to find. Do you think you can do it?

 Why are they together?

 What is this for?

 This looks like a lamp. Do you think that's what it is?

 There are several dogs in this book. Where do you find this one?

 This animal is easy to recognize, but can you find it?

 Don't you think this man is hard working?

 What do you think was in this bag?

 Guess who this belongs to. What is it?

 This pair of shoes belongs on whose feet?

 Can you imagine what this contains?

 Where do you find this tray?

SEEK AND FIND
BIBLE STORIES
THE NEW TESTAMENT

THE NEW TESTAMENT

CONTENTS

The Birth of Jesus

All the people you see here come from the city of Bethlehem (except for Mike—he lives near you). Everybody is in Bethlehem to be counted and registered. Mike is here to see little Jesus. Can you find him? Jesus is God's own Son. Mike knows that, but do you think the others know it?

Questions

1. Where do people go to be registered and counted?

2. No one has counted the sheep. How many are there?

3. Where is the soldier about to lose his spear?

4. Can you see three children going very fast?

5. Do you know why Jesus was born?

Read

Luke 2:1–18

"Today in the town of David a Savior has been born to you; he is Christ the Lord. This will be a sign to you: You will find a baby wrapped in cloths and lying in a manger."

—*Luke 2:11–12*

The Boy Jesus at the Temple

This is the temple in Jerusalem. Jesus is now twelve years old. Sometimes, like today, he is very hard to find. After looking and looking for Jesus, Joseph and Mary have finally found him in the temple. Mike already knew Jesus was here, so he found him first. Jesus was asking the smart men in the temple about God.

Questions

1. What are the people selling?

2. Do you see the boy with a fishing pole?

3. Where is the man telling the people to be quiet?

4. What is the man on the ladder doing?

5. What do you think Jesus and the smart men talked about?

Read

Luke 2:41–49

After three days they found him in the temple courts, sitting among the teachers, listening to them and asking them questions. Everyone who heard him was amazed at his understanding and his answers.

—Luke 2:46–47

The Wedding at Cana

This is quite a wedding Mike is at. It is a big celebration! But they are running out of things to drink. There is Jesus. His mother Mary has asked him to help. So Jesus has asked the servants to pour water into the big, stone water jars. And now Jesus has turned the water into wine. It is his first miracle! Only a couple of people know what has happened. Mike is waiting to see the surprised looks on their faces. He loves parties. He doesn't drink wine, but he would really like some juice.

Questions

1. Where are the two boys feeding a dog?

2. Who is on roller skates?

3. Are the bride and groom in the picture?

4. Where are the servants who are about to drop something?

5. Can you find a child riding a dog?

Read

John 2:1–11

Nearby stood six stone water jars, the kind used by the Jews for ceremonial washing, each holding from twenty to thirty gallons. Jesus said to the servants, "Fill the jars with water"; so they filled them to the brim. Then he told them, "Now draw some out and take it to the master of the banquet." They did so, and the master of the banquet tasted the water that had been turned into wine.

—*John 2:6–9*

Jesus Clears the Temple

Here Mike really finds out just how brave Jesus is. "Get out of here!" he cried at the people who had turned the temple courts into a market. When Jesus started turning over the tables, they could see he was serious. The temple is God's house, built for prayer. It is not to be used to sell things. The disciples look scared. But they know very well that Jesus only does what God wants him to do.

Questions

1. Where is the frightened cow trying to climb a wall?

2. Can you find the alarm clock?

3. Where are the doves coming from?

4. Can you see a violin?

5. Do you see a calculator?

6. How many things and animals are listed in John 2:15–16? (See below.)

Read

John 2:12–21

So he made a whip out of cords, and drove all from the temple area, both sheep and cattle; he scattered the coins of the money changers and overturned their tables. To those who sold doves he said, "Get these out of here! How dare you turn my Father's house into a market!"

—*John 2:15–16*

Jesus Heals a Man Who Cannot Walk

"Just great!" Mike mumbles to himself. He has given up trying to get any closer to Jesus. But the four men have not given up. They want their paralyzed friend to meet Jesus so that he can heal him. That is why they lowered their friend down on his mat. Some people think they have gone too far. Not Jesus. He wants to heal the man. And he does!

Question

1. Do you see a mother holding a rattle for her baby?

2. Which musical instruments can you find?

3. Where is the woman who has lost her yarn?

4. Can you find a boy on a unicycle?

5. Can you find the man who is balancing on a chair?

Read

Mark 2:1–12

"But that you may know that the Son of Man has authority on earth to forgive sins . . ." He said to the paralytic, "I tell you, get up, take your mat and go home." He got up, took his mat and walked out in full view of them all. This amazed everyone and they praised God, saying, "We have never seen anything like this!"

—Mark 2:10–12

The Beatitudes

Now, here there is room enough for everybody, and everybody is listening. Well, almost everybody. A few of the children are not paying attention to Jesus. You can hear him from far away. "Pray," Jesus says, "then you shall be given what you are asking for." Mike thinks to himself, "I've got to remember that."

Questions

1. Can you see any animals here that you have not seen earlier in the book?
2. How many different kinds of birds are there?
3. Can you find a man walking on stilts?
4. Which tree has the most people in it?
5. Which child cannot hear what Jesus is saying?
6. Who is the farthest away from Jesus?

Read

Matthew 4:25–5:12

Now when he saw the crowds, he went up on a mountainside and sat down. His disciples came to him, and he began to teach them, saying:

"Blessed are the poor in spirit, for theirs is the kingdom of heaven."

—*Matthew 5:1–3*

A Sick Woman

Jesus is asking, "Who touched me?" That's why Mike is hiding when Jesus turns around. Is Jesus angry? No, now he tells the woman that she is healed because she believes in Jesus. "I do too," Mike says to himself. He is thankful he is not sick.

Questions

1. Where are the people standing on top of each other?

2. Can you see a boy giving money to a blind beggar?

3. Can you find the man doing handstands on a donkey?

4. Can you find the people standing sideways on a wall?

5. How do you think Jesus healed the woman without even trying?

Read

Mark 5:24–34

At once Jesus realized that power had gone out from him. He turned around in the crowd and asked, "Who touched my clothes?"

"You see the people crowding against you," his disciples answered, "and yet you can ask, 'Who touched me?' "

—Mark 5:30–31

Jesus Feeds the Five Thousand

Mike is thinking to himself, "Isn't this Jesus fantastic?" He saw him take the loaves and the fish into his hands and bless them. Mike was watching very carefully, but he still could not see how Jesus did it. All of a sudden, there is plenty of food—enough for thousands of people. Another miracle!

Questions

1. Who has the most bread?

2. Two people and a cat have already eaten their fish, leaving only the bones. Have you found them?

3. Which toys can you find?

4. Do you think people had balloons at that time?

5. Where is the photographer?

6. Where is Jesus?

Read

Mark 6:30–44

Taking the five loaves and the two fish and looking up to heaven, he gave thanks and broke the loaves. Then he gave them to his disciples to set before the people. He also divided the two fish among them all.

They all ate and were satisfied, and the disciples picked up twelve basketfuls of broken pieces of bread and fish.

The number of the men who had eaten was five thousand.

—Mark 6:41–44

Zacchaeus the Tax Collector

Zacchaeus is a rich tax collector. He is a short man. Look up in the tree, there is Zacchaeus. Can you see him? Mike has spotted him, but he can hardly see Jesus. He hears him though. Jesus calls, "Come down, Zacchaeus, I want to visit you today." How excited Zacchaeus is. He really wants Jesus to visit his home. Jesus teaches Zacchaeus what it means to be a follower of Jesus. And by the end of their visit together, Zacchaeus decides to change his ways from bad to good!

Questions

1. Can you see a turtle?

2. Can you find the two dogs standing on their hind legs?

3. Almost everybody is looking for Jesus or on their way to see him. Can you find anyone who is busy with other things?

4. Where are the two people being carried on stretchers?

Read

Luke 19:1–10

When Jesus reached the spot, he looked up and said to him, "Zacchaeus, come down immediately. I must stay at your house today."

—*Luke 19:5*

The Triumphal Entry

Mike has never seen so many people so excited. Jesus is very popular as he rides into Jerusalem on a donkey. People think he is going to become a king. Mike can hear them calling, "King of Israel!" and "Hosanna!" Mike thinks it sounds great. You can see how the crowd is waving palm branches. Some people have even thrown carpets on the road.

Questions

1. Can you find the street cleaner leaning on his broom?

2. Where is the man in a wheelchair?

3. Can you see a child waving a noisemaker?

4. Have you found the man standing on one arm?

5. How would you welcome Jesus if he came to your neighborhood?

Read

John 12:12–19

The next day the great crowd that had come for the Feast heard that Jesus was on his way to Jerusalem.

They took palm branches and went out to meet him, shouting, "Hosanna!"

"Blessed is he who comes in the name of the Lord!"

"Blessed is the King of Israel!"

—John 12:12–13

The Holy Spirit Comes at Pentecost

Mike is astonished. This is the strangest thing he has ever seen. He knew that Pentecost was about the Holy Spirit. But he didn't know that the Spirit came like fire. Mike can hear the disciples suddenly speaking in different languages. Mike says to Peter, "Do you think that I could receive the Holy Spirit too?"

Questions

1. Can you find the artist painting?

2. Where are the two ladies who are being carried?

3. Can you see a turtle standing on its hind legs?

4. Where is the man riding an ostrich?

5. Have you found the small picture of Jesus on the cross?

6. Did you know Jesus died to save us from our sins?

Read

Acts 2:1–13

Suddenly a sound like the blowing of a violent wind came from heaven and filled the whole house where they were sitting.

They saw what seemed to be tongues of fire that separated and came to rest on each of them.

All of them were filled with the Holy Spirit and began to speak in other tongues as the Spirit enabled them.

—Acts 2:2–4

The Apostles Heal Many

It is obvious to Mike that the disciples have received the Holy Spirit. He watches how all the people around them are being healed. That is why more and more people keep coming. The disciples say that Jesus heals through the Holy Spirit, even though Jesus is in heaven with God. Mike thinks to himself, "That's hard to understand," but he knows deep down it is true.

Questions

1. What is the man on the table doing?

2. Where is the man who can't hear very well?

3. Find the five people walking in single file. Why are they doing that?

4. Can you see some people who have been healed?

5. Can you find a very clever cat?

Read

Acts 5:12–16

As a result, people brought the sick into the streets and laid them on beds and mats so that at least Peter's shadow might fall on some of them as he passed by.

Crowds gathered also from the towns around Jerusalem, bringing their sick and those tormented by evil spirits, and all of them were healed.

—*Acts 5:15–16*

Stephen

How wicked these people are. Stephen has just told them about Jesus, how he was killed on the cross, and now the people are stoning Stephen. Stephen is a martyr, which means someone who dies for his faith in God. Mike has not told anyone that he believes in Jesus. Yet he is afraid that somebody might see him.

Questions

1. How many people are hunting Stephen down?

2. Which of them have rocks in their hands?

3. Who else besides Mike do you think is on Stephen's side?

4. Where is the nest with baby birds?

5. Where are the children?

Read

Acts 6:8–15, 7:54–60

Now Stephen, a man full of God's grace and power, did great wonders and miraculous signs among the people. Opposition arose, however... [The Sanhedrin] were furious and gnashed their teeth at him... They all rushed at him, dragged him out of the city and began to stone him. Meanwhile, the witnesses laid their clothes at the feet of a young man named Saul.

—*Acts 6:8–9, 7:54, 57–58*

The Great Multitude in White Robes

What a party! This is the best party—and the biggest—Mike has ever been to. It is the wedding of the Lamb. Mike knows that the Lamb is Jesus. Everybody is crying out in a loud voice, "Hallelujah! Our Lord God Almighty reigns!" Where is Mike? He is waving his hands and cheering just like the others.

Questions

1. Can you find the angel with no head?

2. Which countries or places in the world do you think these people come from?

3. Where is the man with a beard and glasses?

4. Can you see a man with his right hand over his heart?

5. Do you think we will wear glasses in heaven?

Read

Revelation 19:6–9

Let us rejoice and be glad and give him glory! For the wedding of the Lamb has come, and his bride has made herself ready.

—Revelation 19:7

Here are some of the things Mike found on his journey through the New Testament. Unfortunately, he can't remember where he found them. Can you help him out?

Questions

Guess what this bottle contains. Can you find it?

Can you recognize this bird?

These two small people are far away. Do you think you can find them?

What do you think this is for?

This is a wastebasket. Can you find it?

Obviously, this foot is going somewhere. Do you know where it is?

Where did you see this flag?

Do you recognize this cat?

Where can you find this happy face?

This vase has been knocked down. What happened?

Doesn't that look like a bird? Where is it?

Can you find this face?

This looks like it contains water. Where can you find it?

Doesn't this look like a piece of pottery? Can you find it?